NINETEENTH CENTURY FREEDOM FIGHTERS

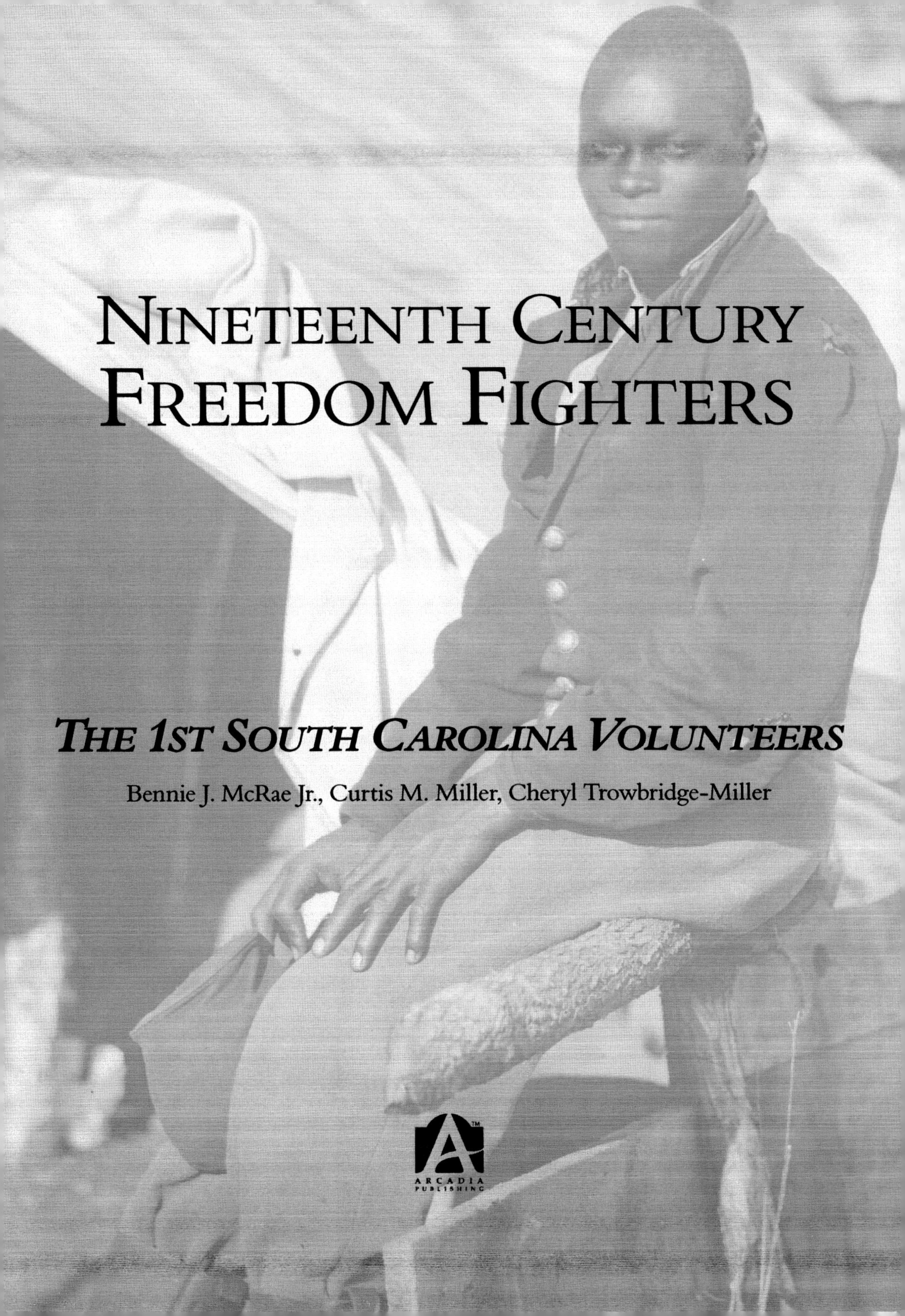

Nineteenth Century Freedom Fighters

The 1st South Carolina Volunteers

Bennie J. McRae Jr., Curtis M. Miller, Cheryl Trowbridge-Miller

Arcadia Publishing

ISBN 978-0-7385-2496-2

Published by Arcadia Publishing,
Charleston SC, Chicago IL, Portsmouth NH, San Francisco CA

Printed in the United States

Library of Congress control number: 2006935744

For all general information contact Arcadia Publishing at:
Telephone 843-853-2070
Fax 843-853-0044
E-Mail sales@arcadiapublishing.com
For customer service and orders:
Toll-Free 1-888-313-2665

Visit us on the Internet at www.arcadiapublishing.com

This book is dedicated to that noble black soldier, Fred Brown.

Special thanks are extended to Daniel W. McQuoid,
the great grandson of Charles Trowbridge, who provided
"everything I have in the hope that one day
his story would be told on a greater scale."

Contents

INTRODUCTION

I have often thought that when the impartial historian shall sit down to write the story of the neglected heroes of the great war for freedom, that he will devote at least one page to this noble black soldier whose conduct on this occasion should give him an honored place among the world's gallant men. Then perhaps the millions of American people who read his story will hang their heads in shame when they recall.

—C. T. Trowbridge

The 1989 film *Glory* dramatized the military career of Col. Robert Gould Shaw and the 54th Massachusetts Infantry, one of the first Union army black units organized in the Northern states. The powerfully portrayed story attracted a broad audience. Many learned for the first time that blacks fought in the Civil War. Undoubtedly, many who saw the film and did no further research believed the 54th was either the only example of blacks as Union soldiers or the first black unit. Neither is true.

The first effort to recruit black soldiers was carried out in May 1862 in South Carolina at the direction of Union general David Hunter, head of the Department of the South. He assigned Sgt. Charles Tyler Trowbridge to recruit the first blacks into the 1st South Carolina Volunteer Infantry. This effort failed in large part because Hunter acted without the authorization of the War Department in Washington, and the regiment was disbanded soon after the initial attempt at organization. Abuses by recruiters other than Trowbridge also contributed to the failure. The 1st South Carolina Volunteers were reorganized in November 1862. Trowbridge was commissioned senior captain of the newly formed regiment, which was later redesignated as the 33rd United States Colored Troops.

Trowbridge's anecdotal memoir, included in this collection, reveals a man who lived out his strong convictions in the leadership of his men. Clearly he was an idealist as well. At the mustering out of the 33rd, he bade farewell to his men, promising that emancipation would reward them with a full share of the benefits of U.S. citizenship and a world of opportunity in their own time. No doubt he wanted those things for the men with whom he had forged relationships. He knew and said that slavery was an abomination. He probably did not realize the profound depth of the wounds the institution had inflicted on a people and the virulence of the bigotry and racism that would frustrate racial reconciliation even into the 21st century.

The character of Colonel Shaw in *Glory* was enhanced with material outside the experiences and biography of the historical figure. At least one of the incidents dramatized in the film is remarkably similar to one related by Trowbridge. Desperately hungry on their march toward mustering out, Trowbridge and his black unit, reaching a Union post, were refused a share of rations that would allow them to continue on. Trowbridge threatened to take the rations by force, and his resolve led to a compromise with the post commander and rations for his men.

Shaw was a courageous man of convictions. He served as the commander of free black men in the Civil War. He died in glory, leading his men into battle at Fort Wagner, South Carolina. He and the 54th Massachusetts Infantry were the natural subject of a Hollywood film.

Trowbridge was also a courageous man of convictions. He served as the commander of former slaves in the Civil War. After the war, he served as an alderman in New York City. In his later years, he was custodian of the Minnesota capitol building. He died of natural causes. Not the stuff of a commercially successful film, but his role in the history of the Civil War and the cause of racial reconciliation sends a fresh message to the 21st century. Racism perpetuates itself through complex social systems, and its eradication is hindered by those systems. But stories of personal triumphs over bigotry and racism still inspire and can provide energy and impetus for the hard work of redesigning those systems to promote and protect reconciliation and human dignity.

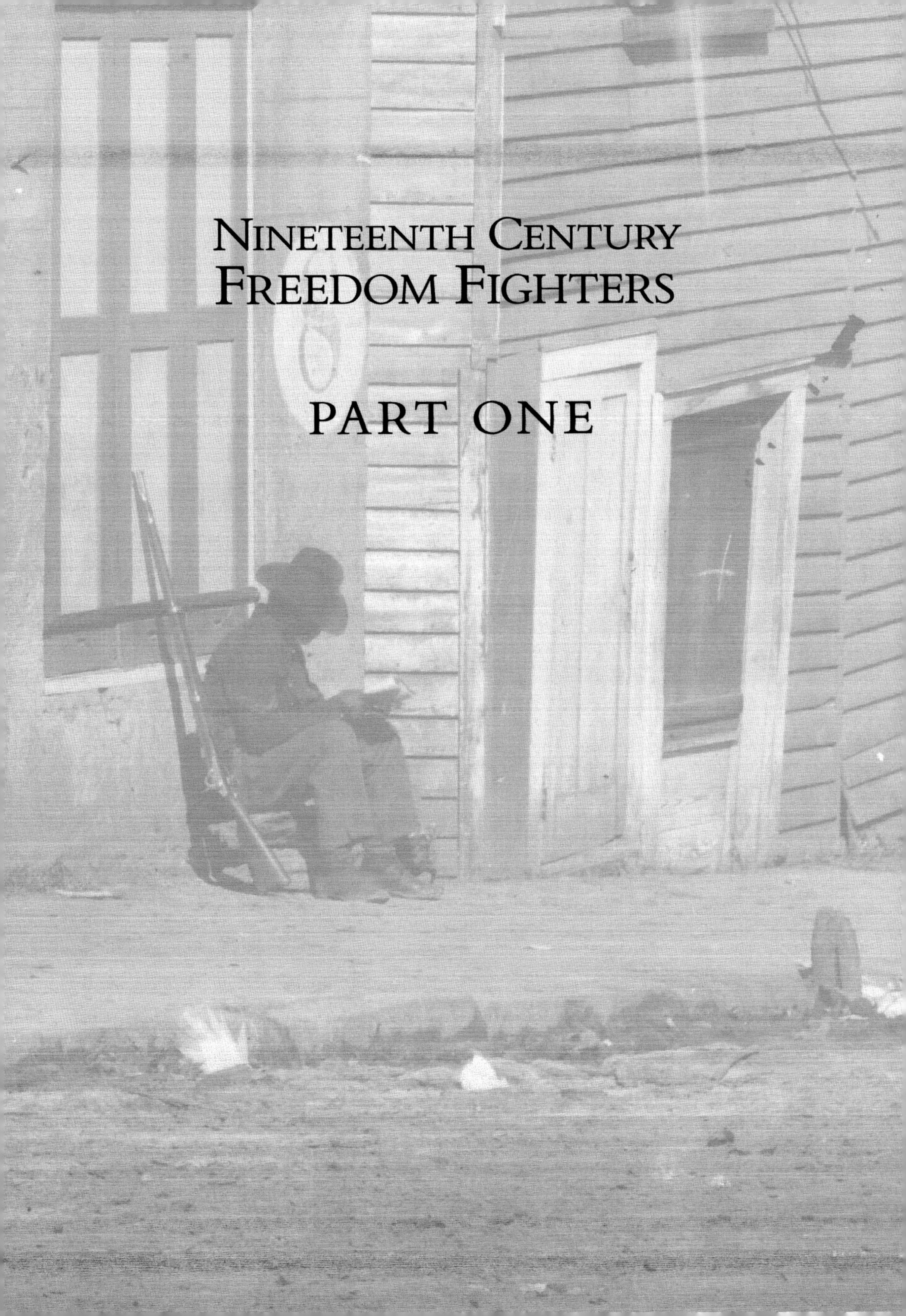

Nineteenth Century Freedom Fighters

PART ONE

1. United States Colored Troops, A Brief History

It is sometimes said that the greatest real heroes of war are the unknown men. . . . There are reported by statistics 178,975 men who served as colored soldiers in our Civil War and the first man who ever enlisted these was Lieutenant Colonel Charles Tyler Trowbridge.

—Col. Thomas Wentworth Higginson, *Boston Transcript*, 1907

Who were the men who made up the United States Colored Troops? Where did they come from? What role did they play in reshaping the social, political, and military structures in the United States of America?

In 1862, Union general David Hunter initiated the first attempt to recruit blacks into the Union army. Congress and the Lincoln White House were chagrined. Hunter had acted on his own, without the blessing of the War Department, Congress, or the president. A member of Congress demanded answers to a series of questions, which had been posed to Hunter by Secretary of War Edwin M. Stanton. In his response to Stanton, Hunter said, in part:

> First, whether I had organized or was organizing a regiment of fugitive slaves . . . I reply that no regiment of "fugitive slaves" has been or is organized in this department. There is, however, a fine regiment of persons whose late masters are "fugitive rebels."

Before Fort Sumter, South Carolina, was fired upon on April 12, 1861, seven states in the South had seceded from the Union. A convention in Montgomery, Alabama, adopted a constitution and elected Jefferson Davis president of the Confederate States of America. In a very short time, four more states seceded: Virginia, Arkansas, Tennessee, and North Carolina. Missouri, Kentucky, Maryland, and Delaware remained in the Union as slave states.

Pres. Abraham Lincoln prepared to put down what he thought would be a minor insurrection with little opposition by blockading Confederate ports and calling for 75,000 volunteers. Thousands flocked to the recruiting centers in the North as well as some areas in the South controlled by federal forces. Among the prospective volunteers were thousands of free blacks in the North and newly escaped slaves in the South. The black men were told that this was a "white man's war" and their services were not needed. Ohio governor David Todd summed up Lincoln's position, stating that "this is a white man's government, they . . . [are] . . . able to defend and protect it."

As both sides developed strategies and drew battle lines during the latter part of 1861 and into 1862, President Lincoln and the War Department realized that they had vastly underestimated the strength and determination of the Confederate forces. Still, they refused to alter the "white man's war" policy. During this period, both sides suffered heavy casualties with the Confederates winning many campaigns. In July 1861, Union forces were defeated at Bull Run (Manassas), Virginia. Less than a month later on August 10, the Confederates recorded yet another victory at Wilson's Creek, in Missouri.

In early 1862, the Confederates claimed a significant victory in the West with the defeat of Union forces at Valerde, New Mexico, on February 21, followed by the near defeat of Union forces under Gen. Ulysses S. Grant on April 6 and 7 at Shiloh Church and Pittsburg Landing, Tennessee. Each side suffered 10,000 casualties, including Confederate general A. S. Johnston. Then came the defeat of Union forces at Shenandoah Valley on May 8 and the single bloodiest day of the war, where both sides fought to a grisly standstill at Antietam. Six thousand were killed and 17,000 wounded.

Throughout this period, President Lincoln steadfastly refused to alter his policy on enlisting men of African descent. He was attempting to preserve the Union while avoiding the question of slavery, and he did not want to alienate the border slave states that remained in the Union. However, groups including some military commanders defied the policy or lack of policy regarding the utilization of a readily available force.

In Cleveland, Ohio, a newly organized military corps of blacks declared that they were ready to do battle "as in times of 1776 and the days of 1812." In New York City, blacks formed a military club. In Cincinnati, Ohio, a pro-slavery city in which prejudice was open and cruel, the Black Brigade was organized but soon disbanded under the pressure of angry whites. The proprietor of the recruiting station was forced to remove the American flag. The proprietor of another meeting place was told by the police, "We want you damned niggers to keep out of this; this is a white man's war."

The most persistent advocate of arming blacks was the outspoken abolitionist Frederick Douglass, arguably the most influential black leader of his day. "Colored men," he complained, "were good enough to fight under Washington, but they are not good enough to fight under McClellan." He further stated, "The side which first summons the Negro to its aid will conquer."

Thousands of fugitive slaves flocked to Union lines wherever federal forces penetrated new areas in the South. Without a general governmental policy, many commanders tried to send the fugitives back to their masters, forbade them to enter Union lines, or permitted masters and their slave catchers to enter Union lines to retrieve their "property."

When fugitive slaves took refuge within the federal lines near Fort Monroe, Virginia, Gen. Benjamin F. Butler learned that they had been used in building Confederate fortifications. He declared them "contrabands of war," a phrase that stuck, and put them to work building Union fortifications for wages. He took the position that he was not obliged to return property to a foreign government. By the end of 1861, numerous ex-slaves were constructing Union fortifications and working as teamsters, cooks, and carpenters.

In the spring of 1862, Gen. David Hunter triggered a controversy that jolted the Confederacy, aroused the ire of the U.S. Congress, and profoundly piqued President Lincoln. Hunter, commander of the Department of the South, issued an "emancipation proclamation" purporting to free all slaves in South Carolina, Georgia, and Florida:

> Headquarters Department of the South
> Hilton Head, S.C., May 9, 1862
>
> General Orders, No. 11:
> The three States of Georgia, Florida, and South Carolina, comprising the Military Department of the South, having deliberately declared themselves no longer under the protection of the United States of America, and having taken up arms against the said United States, it became a military necessity to

declare them under martial law. This was accordingly done on the 25th day of April, 1862. Slavery and martial law in a free country are altogether incompatible. The persons in these three States, Georgia, Florida, and South Carolina, heretofore held as slaves, are therefore declared forever free.

David Hunter
Major-General Commanding
Ed.W. Smith
Acting Assistant Adjutant-General

Less than two weeks later, President Lincoln publicly repudiated Hunter's "emancipation proclamation":

Washington
This nineteenth day of May, in the year of our Lord one thousand eight hundred and sixty-two by the President of the United States of America

A Proclamation:
Whereas there appears in the public prints, what purports to be a proclamation, of Major General Hunter. . . . And whereas the same is producing some excitement, and misunderstanding; therefore I, Abraham Lincoln, President of the United States, proclaim and declare, that the government of the United States, had no knowledge, information, or belief, of an intention on the part of General Hunter to issue such a proclamation; nor has it yet, any authentic information that the document is genuine—And further, that neither General Hunter, nor any other commander, or person, has been authorized by the Government of the United States, to make proclamations declaring the slaves of any State free; and that the supposed proclamation, now in question, whether genuine or false, is altogether void, so far as respects such declaration.

Abraham Lincoln

Lincoln reflected on his counter-proclamation in a July 12, 1862, speech:

> General Hunter is an honest man. He was, and I hope, still is, my friend. I valued him none the less for his agreeing with me in the general wish that all men every where, could be free. He proclaimed all men free within certain states and I repudiated the proclamation. Yet in repudiating it, I gave dissatisfaction, if not offence, to many whose support the country can not afford to lose. And that is not the end of it. The pressure, in this direction, is still upon me, and is increasing.

Shortly after Lincoln's repudiation, General Hunter, without the permission of the War Department, assigned Sgt. Charles Tyler Trowbridge to begin recruiting ex-slaves from the coastal Sea Islands area to form the first regiment of South Carolina volunteers. When word of the plan had spread, Trowbridge was approached by a slave who exclaimed, "Put me down as William Bronson, Number One, African Foundation."

Years later, Trowbridge wrote of Bronson:

> I go often as circumstances permit and drop a rose on the grave. . . . I live over again the scenes of my army life. . . . I shed a tear. . . . I love to linger . . . in the National Cemetery at Beaufort, where sleeps the dust of Sergeant William Bronson. . . . I look out on the magnificent structure that has been builded on the foundation that he laid.

In his post-war memoir *Army Life in a Black Regiment*, Gen. Thomas Higginson wrote:

> To General David Hunter more than to any other one man, is due the credit for the successful entry upon the stage of the Negro as a soldier in this war. In the spring of 1862, he raised and equipped a regiment of Negroes in South Carolina, and when the fact became known in Washington and throughout the country, such a storm was raised about the ears of the administration that they gracefully stood aside and left the

brave general to fight his enemies in the front and rear as best he might. He was quite capable to do both, as it proved.

On June 9, 1862, the U.S. House of Representatives passed a resolution introduced by Charles Anderson Wickliffe of Kentucky. It called upon the secretary of war for facts about the enlistment of black soldiers and by what authority they were carried out.

The secretary of war replied June 14, 1862, disavowing any official knowledge of such a regiment and denying that any authority had been given to create it. He referred the resolution to General Hunter, who was more than happy to oblige with an explanation. Hunter's sardonic reply reveals his disgust with slavery, his disdain for slave owners, and his steadfast resolve to enlist black soldiers:

Headquarters Department of the South
Port Royal S.C., June 23, 1862

Hon. Edwin M. Stanton, Secretary of War
Washington

Sir:
I have the honor to acknowledge the receipt of a communication from the Adjutant-General of the Army, dated June 16, 1862, requesting me to furnish you with the information necessary to answer certain resolutions introduced in the House of Representatives June 9, 1862, on motion of the Hon. Mr. Wickliffe, of Kentucky, their substance being to inquire: First, whether I had organized, or was organizing, a regiment of fugitive slaves in this department; Second, whether any authority had been given to me from the War Department for such organization; and Third, whether I had been furnished by order of the War Department with clothing, uniforms, arms, equipments, etc., for such a force.

Only having received the letter conveying the inquires at a late hour on Saturday night, I urge forward my answer in time for the steamer sailing today (Monday), this haste preventing me from entering as minutely as I could wish upon many points of detail, such as the paramount importance of the subject calls for. But in view of the near termination of the present session of Congress, and the widespread interest which must have been awakened by Mr. Wickliffe's resolution, I prefer sending even this imperfect answer to waiting the period necessary for the collection of fuller and more comprehensive data.

To the first question, therefore, I reply that no regiment of "fugitive slaves" has been or is organized in this department. There is, however, a fine regiment of persons whose late masters are "fugitive rebels," men who everywhere fly before the appearance of the national flag, leaving their servants behind them to shift as best they can for themselves. So far, indeed, are the loyal persons composing this regiment from seeking to avoid the presence of their late owners that they are now, one and all, working with remarkable industry to place themselves in a position to go in full and effective pursuit of their fugacious and traitorous proprietors.

To the second question, I have the honor to answer, that the instructions given to Brig. General W. T. Sherman by the Hon. Simon Cameron, late Secretary of War, and turned over to me by succession for my guidance, do distinctly authorize me to employ all loyal persons offering their services in defense of the Union and for the suppression of this rebellion in any manner I might see fit, or that the circumstances might call for. There is no restriction as to the character or color of the persons who might be employed, or the nature of the employment; whether civil or military, in which their services should be used. I conclude, therefore, that I have been authorized to enlist "fugitive slaves" as soldiers, could any be found in this department.

No such characters have, however, yet appeared within our most advanced pickets, the loyal slaves everywhere remaining on their plantations to welcome us, and supply us with food, labor and information. It is the masters who have, in every instance, been the "fugitives"—running away from loyal slaves as well as loyal soldiers, and whom we have only partially been able to see—chiefly their heads over ramparts, or, rifle in hand, dodging behind trees, in the extreme distance. In the absence of any "fugitive master" law, the deserted slaves would be wholly without remedy, had not the crime of treason given them the right to pursue, capture, and bring back those persons of whose protection they have been thus suddenly bereft.

To the third interrogatory, it is my painful duty to reply, that I never have received any specific authority for issues of clothing, uniforms, arms, equipments, etc., to the troops in question. My general instructions from Mr. Cameron, to employ them in any manner I might find necessary, and the military exigencies of the department and the country being my only, but, in my judgment, sufficient justification. Neither have I had any specific authority for supplying these persons with shovels, spades and pickaxes when employing them as laborers, nor with boats and oars when using them as lightermen: but these are not points included in Mr. Wickliffe's resolution. To me it seemed that liberty to employ men in any particular capacity implied with it liberty also to supply them with the necessary tools; and acting under this faith I have clothed, equipped and armed the only loyal regiment yet raised in South Carolina.

I must say in vindication of my conduct that had it not been for the many other diversified and imperative claims on my time, a much more satisfactory result might have been hoped for; and that, in place of only one, as at present, at least five or six well-drilled, brave, and thoroughly acclimated regiments should by this time have been added to the loyal forces of the Union.

The experiment of arming the blacks, so far as I have made it, has been a complete and even marvelous success. They are sober, docile, attentive, and enthusiastic, displaying great natural capacities for acquiring the duties of a soldier. They are eager beyond all things to take the field and be led into action; and it is the unanimous opinion of the officers who have had charge of them, that in the peculiarities of this climate and country, they will prove invaluable auxiliaries, fully equal to the similar regiments so long and successfully used by the British authorities in the West Indies.

In conclusion I would say it is my hope, there appearing to be no possibility of other reinforcements owing to the exigencies of

> the campaign in the peninsula, to have organized by the end of next fall and to be able to present to the Government from forty-eight to fifty thousand of these hardy and devoted soldiers.
>
> Trusting that this letter may form part of your answer to Mr. Wickliffe's resolution.
>
> I have the honor to be, most respectfully, your obedient servant,
> D. Hunter
> Major General Commanding

Hunter's letter was read aloud in the House and widespread laughter from both sides of the aisle made further action impossible. Years later, Samuel Sullivan "Sunset" Cox, a representative from Ohio present that day, recalled the experience:

> I tell you that letter from Hunter spoiled the prettiest speech I had ever thought of making. I had been delighted with Wickliffe's motion, and thought the reply to it would furnish us with first-rate democratic thunder for the next election. I made up my mind to sail in on Hunter's answer no matter what it was—the moment it came, and to be even more humorously successful in its delivery and reception than I was in my speech against war-horse Gurley of Ohio.
>
> Well you see, man proposes, but Providence orders otherwise. When the clerk announced the receipt of the letter, and that he was about to read it, I caught the Speaker's eye, and was booked for the first speech against your Negro experiment. The first sentence being formal and official was very well: but at the second the House began to grin, and at the third, there was not a man on the floor, except Father Wickliffe, of Kentucky, perhaps, who was not convulsed with laughter. Even my own risibles I found to be affected, and before the document was concluded, I motioned to the Speaker that he might give the floor to whom he pleased, as my desire to distinguish myself in that particular tilt was over.

Hunter's letter angered those who could not fathom calling a slave a soldier in the Union army. President Lincoln and the War Department forced the 1st to disband, with the exception of Trowbridge's Company A. Even then, they were not paid for their service from May 8, 1862, through November 1862.

Early in the fall of 1861, Gov. John Andrew of Massachusetts, a strong abolitionist, declared, "it is not my opinion that our generals, when any man comes to the standard and desires to defend the flag, will find it important to light a candle, and see what his complexion is, or to consult the family Bible to ascertain whether his grandfather came from the banks of the Thames or the banks of the Senegal."

Two years later, when Governor Andrew was preparing to organize the 54th Massachusetts Volunteers (the *Glory* regiment), he sought the advice and counsel of Col. Thomas W. Higginson, commander of the 1st South Carolina Volunteer Infantry:

> Commonwealth of Massachusetts
> Executive Department, Boston, February 5, 1863
>
> To Col. T. W. Higginson
> Commanding 1st Regt. S.C. Vols., Port Royal Island, S.C.
>
> Colonel—
> I am under obligations to you for your very interesting letter of January 19th, which I considered to be too important in its testimony to the efficiency of colored troops to be allowed to remain hidden on my files. I therefore placed some portions of it in the hands of Hon. Stephen M. Weld, of Jamaica Plain, for publication, and you will find enclosed the newspaper slip from the "Journal" of February 3rd, in which it appeared. During a recent visit at Washington I have obtained permission from the Department of War to enlist colored troops as part of the Massachusetts quota, and I am about to begin to organize a colored infantry regiment, to be numbered the "54th Massachusetts Volunteers."
>
> I shall be greatly obliged by any suggestions which your experience may afford concerning it, and I am determined that it shall serve as a model, in the high character of its officers and

> the thorough discipline of its men, for all subsequent corps of the like material.
>
> Please present to General Saxton the assurances of my respectful regard.
>
> I have the honor to be, respectfully and obediently yours,
> John A. Andrew
> Governor of Massachusetts

Frederick Douglass's appeal, "Men of Color, to Arms," argued that "liberty won only by white men would lose half of its luster." Later he insisted that military service offered "a genuine opportunity to achieve first-class citizenship." Douglass and black abolitionists Martin Delany, Henry Highland Garnet, and Charles Lenox Redmond toured the North recruiting to fill the ranks of the 54th Massachusetts Volunteer Infantry Regiment.

The majority of Southern enlistees were illiterate, and their demeanor was best described by an officer in the 1st South Carolina Volunteers:

> The average plantation Negro was a hard-looking specimen, with about as much of the soldier to be seen in him as there was in the angel in Michelangelo's block of marble before he applied his chisel. But, after drilling and teaching, the plantation manners, the awkward bowing and scraping . . . with hat under arm and with averted look, were exchanged for the upright form, the open face, the gentlemanly address, and soldierly salute.

Black soldiers were not welcomed by all of their white Northern comrades. Many white citizens in the North and white Union soldiers were outraged that blacks, especially ex-slaves, were now wearing the uniform of their country. This attitude, coupled with an order from Pres. Jefferson Davis to immediately hang captured black soldiers or white officers leading them, made military life extremely difficult. However, blacks were determined to fight and preserve their freedom at all costs.

When a Jefferson Davis proclamation branded Generals Hunter and Phelps as outlaws and the soldiers under the command of General Butler as robbers and criminals deserving death, Hunter went right to the top with his response:

Hilton Head, Port Royal, S.C., April 25, 1863

Hon. E. M. Stanton,
Secretary of War, Washington:

Sir:
I have the honor to inclose you a copy of a letter to Jefferson Davis.

Hoping it will meet your approval, I have the honor to be, very respectfully, your most obedient,
D. Hunter
Major-General

[Inclosure]
Headquarters Department of the South
Hilton Head, S.C., April 23, 1863

Jefferson Davis, Richmond, Va.:
The United States flag must protect all its defenders, white, black, or yellow. Several Negroes in the employ of the Government in the Western Department have been cruelly murdered by your authorities and others sold into slavery. Each outrage of this kind against the laws of war and humanity which may take place in this department shall be followed by the immediate execution of the rebel of highest rank in my possession. Man for man, these executions will certainly take place for every one sold into slavery worse than death. On your authorities will rest the responsibility of having inaugurated this barbarous policy, and you will be held responsible in this world and in the world to come for all the blood thus shed.

In the month of August last you declared all those engaged in arming the negroes to fight for their country to be felons, and directed the immediate execution of all such as should be captured. I have given you long enough to reflect on your folly. I now give you notice that unless this order is immediately revoked I will at once cause the execution of every rebel officer and every rebel slaveholder in my possession. This sad state of things may be kindly ordered by an all-wise Providence to induce the good people of the North to act earnestly and to realize that they are at war. Thousands of lives may thus be saved.

The poor Negro is fighting for liberty in its truest sense, and Mr. Jefferson has beautifully said, "In such a war there is no attribute of the Almighty which will induce him to fight on the side of the oppressor."

You say you are fighting for liberty. Yes, you are fighting for liberty—liberty to keep 4,000,000 of your fellow-beings in ignorance and degradation; liberty to separate parents and children, husband and wife, brother and sister; liberty to steal the products of their labor, exacted with many a cruel lash and bitter tear; liberty to seduce their wives and daughters, and to sell your own children into bondage; liberty to kill these children with impunity, when the murder cannot be proven by one of pure white blood. This is the kind of liberty—the liberty to do wrong—which Satan, chief of the fallen angels, was contending for when he was cast into hell.

I have the honor to be, very respectfully, your most obedient servant,
D. Hunter
Major-General, Commanding

A turning point for Trowbridge and his men came on February 8, 1864, when the War Department, now willing to call these men soldiers, redesignated the 1st South Carolina Volunteer Infantry as the 33rd U.S. Colored Troops (USCT). (It should be noted that despite redesignation, the men never stopped referring to themselves as "De Fus' Souf," according to Higginson's post-war memoir in the New York newspaper *The Outlook.*) Trowbridge was finally at liberty to correspond with the War Department regarding the achievements of the 33rd USCT on the battlefield:

December 20, 1864—Skirmish near the Pocotaligo Road, S.C.
Report of Col. Edward N. Hallowell, Fifty-fourth Massachusetts Infantry, Commanding Second Brigade, Coast Division

Headquarters Second Brigade, Coast Division
December 21, 1864

I have the honor to report that the Thirty-third U.S. Colored Infantry, Lieut. Col. C. T. Trowbridge commanding, returned last night at 7 o'clock from their reconnaissance. Leaving camp at 3.30 p.m. they proceeded northward and took the direction of the Tullifinny Creek. When about two miles and a half from our lines, the column changed direction to the right, and proceeded in an easterly course till they found an outpost of the enemy. Two companies were detached with a view to capturing the post, but were discovered and the alarm given. The enemy, 300 strong, formed line of battle and made a stand in the skirts of the woods, near the Pocotaligo road, when Lieutenant-Colonel Trowbridge charged them and drove them back into the woods on the right. We here captured some of their blankets, overcoats, haversacks, canteens, &c., and then moved down the Pocotaligo road to camp. Our casualties in this action are 7 wounded, 1 mortally; no prisoners were captured, and the loss of the enemy is not known. Inclosed is Lieutenant-Colonel Trowbridge's report, including a nominal list of casualties.

First Lieut. C. H. Robbins, Twenty-sixth U.S. Colored Troops, accompanied Lieutenant-Colonel Trowbridge, and rendered very valuable services as guide.

I am, sir, respectfully, your obedient servant,
E. N. Hallowell
Colonel, Commanding Second Brigade
Lieut. L. B. Perry
Acting Assistant Adjutant-General

December 20, 1864—Skirmish near the Pocotaligo Road, S.C.
Report of Lieut. Col. Charles T. Trowbridge, Thirty-third U. S. Colored Troops.

Headquarters Thirty-third U.S. Colored Troops

In the Field, December 21, 1864

Lieutenant:
I have the honor to report that, in accordance with instructions received from the colonel commanding brigade, I proceeded at 3.30 p.m. yesterday, the 20th, with 300 men of my command, along the right bank of the Tullifinny to a point two miles beyond our picket-line; then turned to the right and endeavored to strike the Pocotaligo road, a mile beyond the plantation house known as the Thomas Stewart place. When within three-quarters of a mile of the Pocotaligo road I encountered a strong cavalry picket line of the enemy, apparently so posted that his left rested on the Pocotaligo River, his right reaching around to a swamp on the west side of the road and nearly a mile from it. As soon as I encountered the picket I ordered a halt and sent two companies, under the command of Major Whitney, who were ordered to get between the enemy's pickets and the swamp and capture them if possible; but in so doing they were discovered and fired upon by the enemy. They returned the fire, gave the alarm, and immediately the enemy's picket-line retired to their reserves, dismounted, formed line of battle, apparently 300 strong, under cover of the woods in my front, and opened a brisk fire on my men. I then sent forward a company of skirmishers to engage the enemy until the two companies under Major Whitney had rejoined the main column. I then formed line of battle and charged across the open field into the woods and routed the enemy, who broke and fled in the direction of the railroad. The number of the enemy killed or wounded is not known, but one killed was found on the field: but from the number of haversacks, blankets, and forage (all of which was destroyed on the field or brought away), their loss must have been considerable. The enemy had no artillery, but their cavalry horses are apparently very fine and the men armed with good carbines. My casualties were 7 enlisted men wounded, 4 seriously and 3 slightly.

My observations yesterday have convinced me that the only way to reach the railroad with a force from our present position is by the way of the Pocotaligo road, as the country on our left is full of swamps, which are impassable for anything except light troops. The Pocotaligo road between our intrenchments and the Stewart plantation I found obstructed in three places by felled trees.

My thanks are due to Lieutenant Robbins, of the Twenty-sixth U.S. Colored Troops, who proved himself to be a brave and efficient officer.

I am, sir, very respectfully, your obedient servant,
C. T. Trowbridge
Lieutenant-Colonel, Commanding Regiment
Lieut. George F. McKay
Acting Assistant Adjutant-General

2. Charles Tyler Trowbridge

Because of the differences personally, professionally, intellectually, and culturally the officers of black troops seldom kept in touch. Charles Trowbridge was the exception.

—Joseph T. Glatthaar,
The Civil War Alliance of Black Soldiers and White Officers

Charles Tyler Trowbridge was born January 10, 1835, in Morristown, New Jersey, in an area known as Trowbridge Mountain. He was third of seven children born to Elijah Freeman Trowbridge and Temperance Ludlow Muchmore.

He moved to Brooklyn, New York, with his parents in 1854. On March 11, 1857, he married Emeline Haviland Jackson at Freehold, New Jersey. They had one child, Ida Emeline Trowbridge, on April 8, 1858. Emeline died November 24, 1858.

Charles enlisted in the 1st New York Engineers, Company F, on December 4, 1861. On December 15, 1861, he married his second wife, Jane Pooler Martin, in Brooklyn. A short time later, he was promoted to sergeant and was assigned as orderly to Gen. David Hunter, commander of the Department of the South, Union army.

Sergeant Trowbridge was reassigned to the 1st South Carolina Volunteers under General Hunter when the regiment was first organized in May 1862. At the same time, Hunter declared martial law and freedom for all blacks in Union-held territories. In part because the orders had been given without authority from the War Department, Lincoln rescinded Hunter's orders, and the unit was disbanded in August 1862. The policy at the time stated that no black soldiers were needed or wanted in the Union army. Additionally, the Confederate congress accused Lincoln of exciting Negro insurrection and issued orders that officers of colored regiments be put to death.

The 1st South Carolina Volunteers reorganized in November 1862, and Sergeant Trowbridge was commissioned captain.

In August 1863, Trowbridge was promoted to the rank of major. He was known to have had daily devotion with the regiment, and it is said that he gave his men speeches on the equality of the races in which he told them they should not allow themselves to be considered less than equal.

In May 1864, Col. Thomas W. Higginson left the regiment due to injuries received at Edisto Island, South Carolina. At this time, the command was officially given to Col. W. F. Bennett, but for reasons not clear in the record, it was Major Trowbridge who actually commanded the regiment at that time and until it mustered out. He was promoted to lieutenant colonel, his highest rank, on December 9, 1864. It was said that he did not have the education that the War Department deemed adequate for promotion to colonel.

Susie King Taylor wrote in *A Black Woman's Civil War Memoirs*, "He was greatly admired by his troops. No officer in the army was more beloved than our Lieutenant-Colonel C. T. Trowbridge." This was no doubt due, at least in part, to his refusal to leave his troops when his tour of duty was over.

Taylor also indicated that despite the disbanding of Company A in May 1862, the men never stopped being soldiers, and, by the time the regiment was legally organized, all the men knew of Charles Trowbridge and wanted to be in his company. This included her husband, Edward King, of Company E, who expressed disappointment in not being assigned to Company A. She further states that he visited all of his men in their tents before they came under his command and assigned her to teach any that were interested in learning to read and write.

Taylor also wrote of the general orders to muster out, "They were delighted to go home, but oh! how they hated to part from their commanding chief, Colonel C.T. Trowbridge. He was the very first officer to take charge of black soldiers. We thought there was no one like him."

3. The Return of the Ransomed

Two colored sergeants were examined by a committee appointed by Gen. Gilmore for the position of lieutenant, to which they had been recommended by their generous lieutenant, Charles T. Trowbridge. They were opposed by Col. Bennett and the post-commander; Gen. Grover, on the ground that it was not the policy of the Government to commission colored men. The question was submitted to the decision of Gen. Gilmore, commander of the district, who returned answer that he would appoint a committee to examine the young sergeants, and if found competent their color should be no bar to their promotion. Lieut. Trowbridge was nervous with anxiety about their success, not only because his reputation was at stake, but because he desired the principle involved to be triumphant. Never was an officer more enthusiastic about his regiment than this magnanimous man. "Not color of the skin, but manhood," was his motto. Would to God that the army and the nation had been ruled by such men!

—Bishop Daniel Alexander Payne, D.D., LL.D.

In the years following the war and his duty in post-war South Carolina, Trowbridge recalled in memoirs his experiences on both sides of the surrender at Appomattox. In this recollection, Trowbridge tells of the Reverend Daniel Alexander Payne's visit to the 33rd USCT just as the official end of the war had been announced.

> I little thought when the march to the Sea was over, and Sherman had presented the city of Savannah, with all it contained to President Lincoln as a Christmas present, that it would fall to my lot to take quite an active part in the government of that fair city after Sherman had marched on to Raleigh. But such was the case.
>
> I entered the city of Savannah March 11th 1865, remaining there till the middle of June. My regiment did provost guard

duty in all parts of the city, and during my term of service there the following interesting incident occurred.

It was the visit of Bishop D. A. Payne of the African Methodist Episcopal Church to the South for the first time in Thirty Five years. He having made his escape from Slavery at Charleston S.C. when a small boy. He reached the North, secured a fair education and became a noted minister in his church. Of course he was denied the privilege of returning to his old home until after the war, and was in Savannah at the funeral services of President Lincoln. He had known of my work among the slaves, in introducing them into the army as soldiers, and sent me a note expressing his great desire to see my regiment. I accordingly set a time which would be most convenient for both him and the men. You must bear in mind that my regiment was the first black regiment in the war, and composed exclusively of slaves. I had taken special pains to see that the regiment was kept in the best of order as far as dress, discipline, and efficiency were concerned. I had erected a temporary school house and appointed such teachers as I could get to teach the men the rudiments of an education. Over the door of the school room I had placed a pair of stocks which I had secured from the jail where the slaves were sent to be whipped. The school was so situated that it was in full view from the line of review. At the time appointed the regiment was paraded, and all companies equalized so that I could maneuver them with perfect military precision. At the close of the parade I walked with the Bishop to my proper station, and after a short drill in the manual of arms, I gave the necessary command to form a Hollow Square by the Double Quick movement and then invited the Bishop to step inside the square. When the men had uncovered their heads I turned to introduce the Bishop and found him weeping like a child. His great soul was running over with an irrepressible gratitude to God as he beheld the Morning of Freedom after the night of bondage and sorrow had passed. Some moments elapsed before he became sufficiently composed to reply to my introduction. He began in a voice full of pathos and eloquence such as I have never listened to either before or since.

He talked of the wrongs and the sufferings that his race had so painfully endured for centuries; of the heart rending separations when mothers and children had been torn from each other's embrace and dragged to the auction block to be sold like a beast of the stall. He then called upon the men of the regiment to render thanksgiving to the Father of us all who had in the far off long ago appointed Moses to lead the children of Israel out of Egyptian bondage; so likewise he had appointed Abraham Lincoln to lead the black race out of the bondage of slavery into the promised land of Liberty.

Then pointing to the school house over the door of which the broken stocks in whose cruel shackles their bleeding forms had so often been firmly bound while their quivering flesh had been beaten with many stripes, said, but at last the day of our deliverance has come. The last shackle has been broken; the last slave has been set at liberty. Hence forth the church, the school house, our wives, and our children are our own forevermore. He exhorted them to enter into the new life before them with songs of rejoicing, with full purpose of heart to prove themselves worthy of their exalted citizenship into which they had come.

Then in closing he reminded them that the Moses that led God's ancient children, had been denied the joy of entering the promised land. He died, and God buried him, no man knowing where his sepulcher is. But our Abraham found a burial place where all men of every nation can do him homage. And he is embalmed in the hearts of sixty millions of American Freemen.

The square was then reduced, the parade dismissed and a thousand happy black soldiers repaired to their tents for the night. With the Bishop on my arm as we left this never to be forgotten scene, he said to me "Col. surely we have lived to see fulfilled that day long since foretold when a nation shall be born in a day."

I have so often wished that I had the power to describe that scene. When the speech was done, tears were everywhere. Hearts that had never known much of joy were now bounding with irrepressible expressions of delight. Faces that long years

> of wearisome, unrequited toil had rendered sad and defeated were now wreathed in smiles like the shining bosom of Galilee when the divine Master said Peace —be still. I do not pretend to reproduce this memorable speech, but to have been present, and to have been an actor in this scene, I have always regarded as one of the greatest privileges that ever came to my lot to enjoy. I would have rather been an actor in the scene I have described than to have stood where God's brightest Angels stood when He spoke this world from naught and threw it out of the window of Creation and sent it bowling along the galleries of the skies. For in that day we joined with Wm. Lloyd Garrison, the great Champion of human liberty in his farewell as Editor of the Liberator. . . . Hail ye ransomed millions.

Even when Gen. Robert E. Lee surrendered at Appomattox in April 1865, the work of the 33rd USCT was far from over. Trowbridge and his regiment had important work to do in executing Union policy in the still hostile territory of South Carolina under the aegis of the Freedman's Bureau.

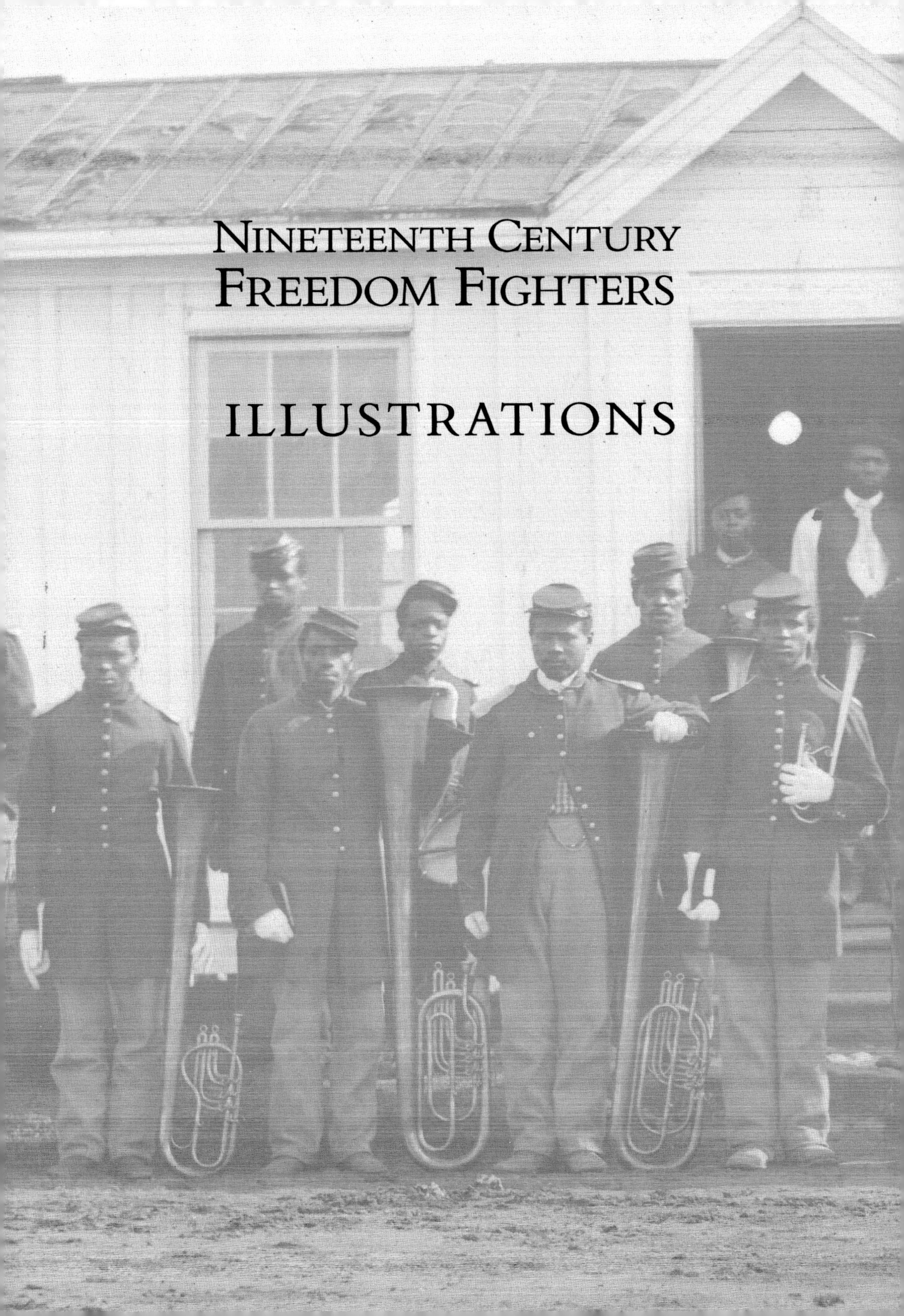

Nineteenth Century Freedom Fighters

ILLUSTRATIONS

Pictured is Maj. Gen. David Hunter, Union commander of the South, who assigned Sgt. Charles Tyler Trowbridge to recruit the first blacks into the 1st South Carolina Volunteer Infantry.

Slaves were bought and sold throughout the South. This photograph shows a black Union soldier sitting outside one such establishment in Atlanta.

CHINA, GLASS
&
QUEENSWARE
F. GEUTEBRUCK.
AUCTION & NEGRO SALES.
ATLANTA
CIGAR
MANUFACTORY
CIGARS & TOBACCO

This typical slave pen was located in Alexandria, Virginia.

These slaves were photographed at the Smith plantation on Port Royal Island in South Carolina.

Slaves prepare cotton for the gin on the Smith plantation on Port Royal Island in South Carolina.

These escaped slaves were photographed at a Virginia farm where the Union's secret service stayed in May 1862.

383

Many freed and escaped slaves, like these pictured with all their possessions loaded in a wagon, fled to Union lines with their families.

Shown here is the interior of Fort Sumter, located in Charleston, South Carolina, with gabion reinforcements.

Fearing that the Confederacy would take control of the facility, the Union shipyard commander ordered the burning of the navy shipyard in Norfolk, Virginia. Seen here is the aftermath of the destruction.

This row of stacked federal rifles in Petersburg, Virginia, was part of military drills and ceremonies aptly called "stacking rifles."

"And when I go through South Carolina it will be one of the most horrible things in the history of the world." The proof of Sherman's resolve is evident in this photograph of the ruins of the North Eastern Railroad depot in Charleston.

3082

Sherman's march destroyed hundreds of miles of railroads. Pictured here is a crippled locomotive at the Richmond and Petersburg Railroad depot.

This photograph shows wheels and burned railroad cars near a Richmond and Petersburg Railroad station, a common sight throughout the Confederate states.

19

"The devil himself couldn't restrain my men in that state," Sherman said of South Carolina. Depicted is Charleston's Mills House Hotel, with adjacent ruins. The hotel was built in 1853 and was scarred by fire during the war but not destroyed.

These houses, located on the Battery in Charleston, South Carolina, were damaged by shellfire.

3451

This view depicts war-ruined buildings in Charleston, South Carolina.

Federal soldiers rebuild the Orange and Alexandria Railroad bridge over Cedar Run in the vicinity of Catlett's Station, Virginia.

The 1st South Carolina Volunteers were photographed on dress parade to hear the reading of Lincoln's Emancipation Proclamation on January 1, 1863.

Soldiers from the 33rd USCT, formerly known as the 1st South Carolina Volunteers, sit outside the bombproof quarters of Major John D. Strong at Dutch Gap, Virginia, in July 1864.

Before African Americans were found to be "good enough to fight," they were allowed to help by burying the dead. Here, black soldiers collect the bones of soldiers killed in the battle of Cold Harbor, Virginia.

During the early years, blacks were frequently given tasks such as cooking, cleaning, and carpentry. In this image, an army cook was photographed at work in City Point, Virginia.

Soldiers of the United States Colored Troops unload a ship in City Point, Virginia, the home of General Grant's headquarters.

2457

These seven "contrabands" are dressed in old Union uniforms and stand in front of a wagon and shack. Gen. Benjamin F. Butler coined the term contraband to describe runaway slaves in the Union army.

Men of the 107th U.S. Colored Infantry were photographed standing with their musical instruments in hand.

Band 107 Col Troops Ft Corcoran Nov 1865 W M S No. 861

William Johnson, a black soldier, was executed by hanging, bringing to mind the words of C. T. Trowbridge: "In the event of any one of us that might be captured we would have no other hope than instant death by hanging."

Two soldiers of the 23rd New York Infantry, one black and one white, are pictured here smoking a long pipe in front of tent.

Two members of the U.S. Colored Troops take a relaxing break from army life in Culpeper, Virginia.

Two black soldiers posed for this photograph with Capt. James M. Robertson and his staff at Brady Station, Virginia, the headquarters of the 1st Brigade, Horse Artillery.

These unidentified black soldiers rest near the Aiken house in Virginia.

These Union soldiers were photographed at Catlett's Station, Virginia. Several soldiers rest in and on top of the U.S. military railroad boxcars.

The federal cavalry guard a depot and boxcars in Chattanooga, Tennessee.

NINETEENTH CENTURY FREEDOM FIGHTERS

PART TWO

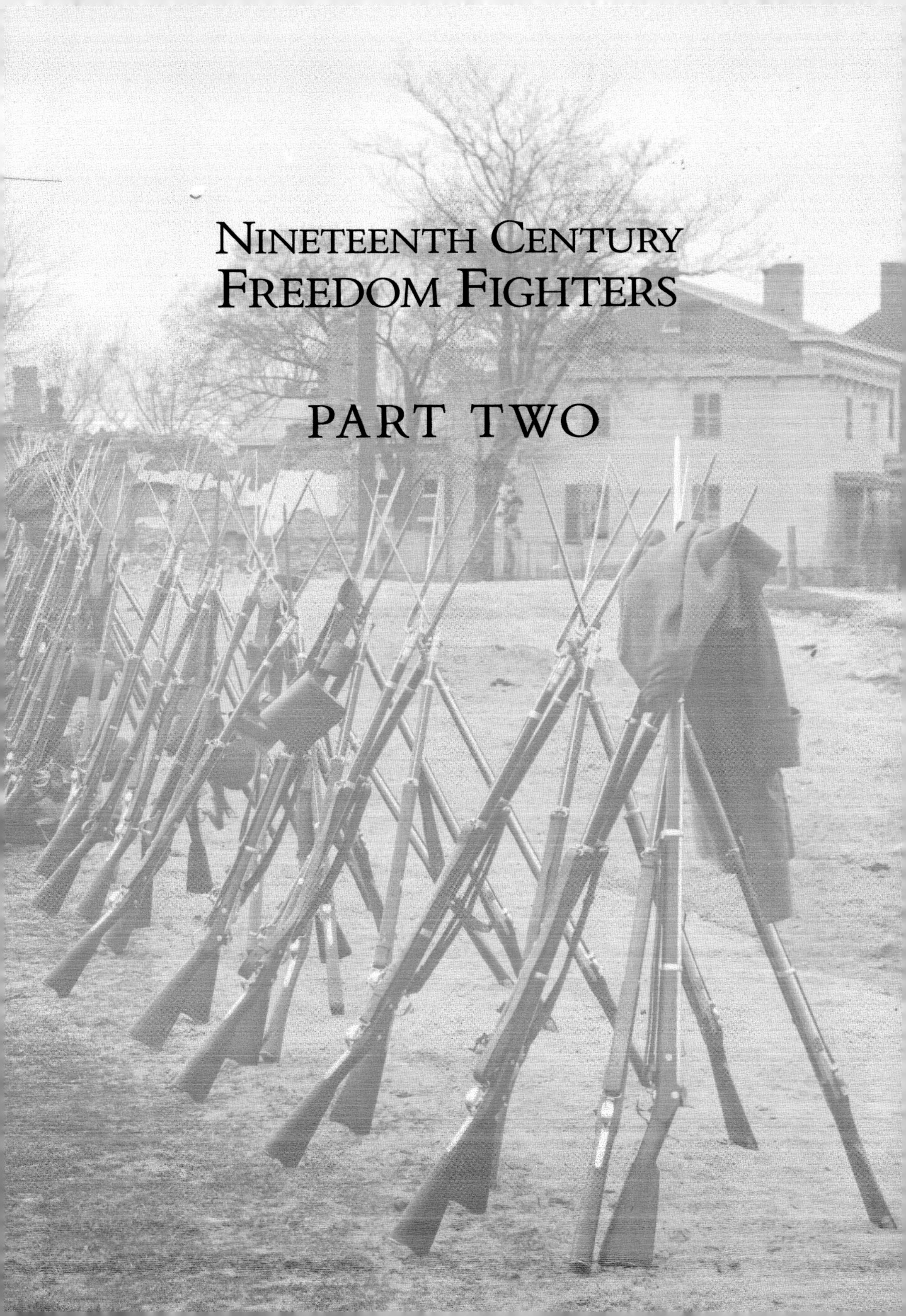

On March 3, 1865, Congress established the Bureau of Refugees, Freedmen, and Abandoned Lands. The chief work of the Freedman's Bureau, as it was more commonly known, fell into five categories: relief work for blacks and whites in war-devastated areas, regulation of post-slavery black labor, justice administration in cases involving blacks, management of abandoned and confiscated property, and the support of education for blacks. Congress intended the bureau "to continue during the present war of rebellion, and for one year thereafter."

The bureau was organized under the War Department, and Gen. Oliver O. Howard was named its commissioner. Backed by military force, the bureau was one of the most powerful agencies of Reconstruction. The act that created the bureau provided that "any military officer may be detailed and assigned to duty under this act without increase of pay or allowances." It was under that provision that Lt. Col. Charles Trowbridge and his regiment of the 33rd USCT were assigned to provide military support to Freedman's Bureau activities in South Carolina.

In the following pages, Trowbridge relates his experiences in the bureau in his own words.

4. Experiences in the Freedman's Bureau, South Carolina

by C. T. Trowbridge

What was to be done for or with the Negro now that he is free was the question that confronted this country at the close of the war, and that question brought into existence what was known as the Freedman's Bureau and to that branch of the service I was assigned with my regiment in July 1865, and given command of what was known as the sub-district of Northwestern South Carolina which embraced the counties of Pickens and Anderson with headquarters at the Anderson Court House.

Anderson County cast 2,400 votes in favor of carrying the Ordinance of Secession and there were 1,800 either killed or wounded in the Confederate army before the surrender. There was a large population of freed slaves who were very poor and destitute of clothing and who were most thoroughly hated by the whites who had owned them prior to the war. You will readily see that for me to take a regiment of black soldiers into this community and begin the work of organizing a form of government—that should require the Negro to stay on the plantation where he had been born, and work for his former master, and require the old master to treat him humanely—not to say kindly—was a work that taxed my skill as an executive officer.

In order to reach my new station I was obliged to march from Hamburg, SC northward across that portion of the country that had been traversed by Sherman in his march to the sea. It had been overrun by the Cavalry in the search for Jefferson Davis so that the railroad was for miles destroyed, bridges burned; and all kinds of forage or provisions had been consumed, so that it was little better than a desert.

When we came in sight of the town where we were to make our headquarters we were met by a committee of its citizens who implored me not to "bring them niggers into their town." I saw at once that I had to take my stand, be very stern and resolute or my authority as the Commander of the district would soon be defied. I told them that these men were not "niggers," but United States Soldiers, and that I should march into town and quarter my troops in the courthouse. The length of time that they would remain there would depend entirely upon the conduct of the townspeople themselves toward the men and their Officers. Before night I had taken possession of the Courthouse, had posted a guard in the principal streets of the town, and taken up my own room in the Benson house, the only Hotel in the place.

I began my duties by assigning Captain Sampson as Provost Marshal in an office building convenient to the courthouse, where all the returned Confederate soldiers were required to come and take the oath of allegiance to the United States government. One of the first persons to present himself was Captain John C. Calhoun, grandson of the Great Nullifier of South Carolina. I had met this ardent secessionist some two years before under a flag of truce at Port Royal Ferry, SC. He had repeatedly declined to hold any communication with me because all Southern officers had refused to recognize an officer who commanded colored soldiers. But in this particular instance some of my men had captured a number of his company in one of their night expeditions over on the mainland.

The purpose of this meeting was to bring some clothing and such other comforts as they might need before being sent north as prisoners of war. When they appeared on the opposite bank of the river, they asked to have a boat sent over for them as they were willing to waive their objections to me as a commander of black soldiers. A boat was sent and Captain Calhoun with two other officers were brought to our side of the river.

When we had transacted the business for which the meeting was sought, we sat down for a little chat as to the probable length of time that would elapse before the end of the war would come. He said to me in that haughty southern style, "Major, your fathers and mine did the talking and it remains for you and me to fight, and the south will fight as long as there is a man left to shoot a gun." He then politely requested me to return him to his own side of the river, which request I at once complied with.

His appearance at the office of my provost marshal was the first time we had met after the surrender of Gen. Lee. He at once recognized me and said, "Colonel, I have come to take the d___d Yankee oath." He was told to hold up his hand and be sworn. This done, he turned to me and said, "Now I am as good a Yankee as you are, but I hate you worse than I ever did. Let's go and have a drink." This courtesy I declined with all the politeness of which

I was capable. Our interview closed by his inviting me to his plantation to dine with him as soon as I could find it convenient to do so. The only condition being that when I came I was not to talk politics. I never saw him again, but I have no doubt but what if I could have found the time to have visited him, I should have been treated with the utmost kindness and hospitality for he was a true Southern gentleman; and I would have been made most welcome to the best that he had.

I found as the days passed that there was at that time so much uncertainty as to what the policy of the government would be towards the leading men of the South, that many of this class went into hiding and kept out of reach of those who were charged with the duties of Reconstruction until they could be assured that the government was disposed to be lenient and conciliatory towards them. This fear and distrust gradually wore away as they came to understand that I was their friend and only intended to help those who were really willing to accept the situation in good faith and would yield a willing obedience to the rules the government had prescribed for their conduct and to require a strict obedience from the lawless and disobedient.

In a few days no less a person than the Hon. James L. Orr, who had at one time, before the war, been Speaker of the House of Representatives, called on me and asked what he could do to help repair the damage he had been doing for so many years. I told him that if he would go to Washington, get his political disabilities removed, come back to South Carolina, loyally lending his best efforts to the government, and take a leading part in the cause of reconstruction, we would make him Governor of the State. Acting upon my suggestion, he left for Washington, secured his pardon from President Johnson and returned to his home and set about the work we had in hand.

I together with Captain Sampson and Lieut. White were invited to his house to dine with him. While at dinner he said to me, "Colonel, you and I ought to be friends, for while I was Senator in the Confederate Senate I defended you. I will show you the notes of a speech I made while the question of officers of Negro troops in the Union army was under discussion. Mr. Davis, our president, wanted a law enacted declaring all such persons outlaws and demanding that they be turned over to the State Courts and punished for inciting Negro insurrection according to the laws in the south before the war."

Mr. Orr's contention was, that for the south to enact such a law would be to introduce a new principle in international law not recognized by any nation on earth. If they should presume to dictate to a power that might be at war with them, as to what the color of a soldier's skin should be, it would most assuredly militate against them as a young nation just struggling for recognition as a nation among the other nations of the world. As the question had never before been raised, his advice was for them to wait until their independence had been secured. His colleague, Barwell Rhett, took the opposite view and advocated the speedy passage of the measure and it became a law.

Mr. Orr was a most cordial and very entertaining host, giving us the best that his impoverished condition could afford; only complaining that his servants had all left him since the proclamation of freedom. The white ladies of the household were doing their own work, including cooking, an experience entirely new to the ladies of the South. From that time on Mr. Orr and myself were on terms of great friendship and he rendered me such valuable aid while I remained in command of the district.

I found in the two counties assigned me a large number of persons engaged in distilling a very poor article of what they called peach brandy, which they made in very rude stills from the fruits that grew quite abundantly in all parts of that mountainous region. In order that I could guard against the danger of my soldiers getting this stuff and drinking to excess, an order was issued requiring all persons engaged in this kind of business to report to me for a license, which I was willing to grant without expense to them. This brought to my headquarters within a day or two, a crowd of the most forbidding looking outlaws I had ever met. Each one had with him a large keg or demijohn of the vilest whiskey that man ever drank, wishing me to accept it in payment for their license, protesting that, that alone was all they had to pay with. Each man received his license and a peremptory order to take their stuff out of the town and under no condition was a drop to be sold to the enlisted men of the regiment under penalty of having their license revoked. I am glad to say that I never heard of a single instance in which the order was disobeyed and we had no annoyance from drunkenness while we remained in that country.

Within a day or two after my arrival at Anderson, I received a request to send a company of men to the town of Walhalla some forty miles north as there was much lawlessness and confusion in the place. I at once ordered Captain Parker with his company, in connection with Lieutenant Jerome B. Furman, to march to that point. From information I had of the character of the people, I was most careful to instruct the officers to exercise great watchfulness for a few days and not expose themselves or their men, but to keep quietly in their quarters, and to feel their way, trusting no man who might call on them unless it be the mayor or city councilman. They reached the town partly by marching and partly by using as much of the railroad as had been repaired. They took up their quarters in the principal hotel and set to work making themselves as comfortable as possible.

As night came on, and the evening meal was over, Lieut. Furman stepped out on the front porch when a tall villainous looking ex-confederate stepped up, bade him good evening and said, "We are glad to have you come into our town, for we are absolutely without any kind of government. The town is full of desperate characters; we are living in constant fear of our lives and the presence of United States troops will no doubt soon restore order and be a blessing to us." His mode of speech and cordial manner completely threw the officer off his guard and he foolishly accepted an invitation to take a walk with his newly found acquaintance. They had only walked a few steps before this villain drew his revolver, shot the officer in the back, and as he fell to the ground, he put the muzzle of his pistol to the head of a dying man and discharged two more bullets into his brain, disappearing in the darkness. I was at once sent for with a request to bring more troops. I immediately started with another company as fast as the cars would carry me.

Upon my arrival in the town I sent for the Mayor, took him into the room where the body of the Lieutenant lay and said to him, "As this officer has been murdered I shall hold you responsible for his death, giving you ten hours to produce the murderer or I will burn the town." I instructed him to go to the town hall, ring the bell, call the people together, and state to them what I had told him. This he rather reluctantly complied with, and in a few hours returned saying that the people knew the man, but he was such a desperado that it was more than any man's life was worth to reveal it. I persisted until he gave me the name of the man. I offered a reward of two thousand dollars for his body, dead or alive. I got the citizens to paste the notice of the reward in all parts of the town. This action compelled the people to rely on me for protection from this notorious outlaw. They were from that moment, whether willing or not, very friendly to me.

At the funeral of my dear Comrade, which was held the next day, the entire community turned out, and I have never seen more flowers or any more genuine expressions of sorrow than I witnessed at the burial of this gallant young Officer who was laid in his last resting place at the foot of the mountain where he sleeps in an unmarked grave and is the only Union soldier that I know of in that far away southern village. We knew nothing of his relatives who were supposed to reside in Pennsylvania. I believe his accounts have never been settled with the government to this very day.

Being satisfied in my own mind from what I gathered during the day that the man I was looking for was not in that town, and finding the people entirely willing to assist me in any way in their power to capture the perpetrator of this foul deed, I took a locomotive and returned to my headquarters at Anderson, leaving instructions that any information that might come in should be forwarded to me at once. This was on Thursday, and on the next day a courier arrived saying that the man we wanted would be at church on Sunday at a little meeting house about 12 miles from Anderson.

A description of a roan horse that he was riding when he was last seen was given. I at once dispatched Lieut. Searles with nine mounted men and instructed him to secret his men and horses in a cornfield that I had been told was very near the church. So as darkness came on he moved with great care, got his men in hiding and in the afternoon of Sunday the Roan horse and rider appeared. The horse was tied to the fence and as soon as the man entered the church a dash was made for the horse, which being secured, they made for the door of the church to capture the rider. He however, being on the alert jumped out of a window and made his escape into the cornfield where all track of him was soon lost, and the Lieutenant and his men returned to Anderson with the captured horse.

That night just after midnight I heard a sound of horsemen in the street under my window and shortly a sound of footsteps in the hallway leading to my room was heard, as if someone was coming in their bare feet. As soon as the person came to the door I found it to be an old colored woman who said in a low tone, "Don't go out of this room tonight for Mance Jolly is out there to kill you." She then disappeared as mysteriously as she had come.

A moment later I heard the tramp of three men approaching from the other end of the hallway. These three I took to be the party who were looking for me so I determined to give them a warm reception. Planting myself in front of the door of my room, I listened for them to make a demand upon me to open the door when I would shoot through the panel. To my great joy it turned out to be three of my own officers who had been warned, by the same old colored woman, of my danger and had come to caution me not to expose myself at the window for they would shoot me on sight from the street. Very soon the alarm that the woman had given me reaching the provost guard house, the guard came on the double quick and the rebels hastily rode out of town.

Next morning I had an engagement to meet the colored people on a plantation about three miles out of town for the purpose of arranging a contract between them and a Mr. Crawford Keyes, who had been their former owner, as to the wages he was to pay them and requiring the negros to remain for a year in his employ. I was told by a number of people not to go alone as Jolly would most likely be looking for me. I determined to take with me a man who had been Sheriff at Anderson County and was now a wounded ex-confederate Soldier, by the name of Magee, who knew everybody in that country. He at first declined to go with me saying that undoubtedly Jolly was hiding near the town and as he was such a desperate character, he would kill me as sure as he saw me. I insisted and he at last, very reluctantly, accompanied me.

The weather was terribly hot so we started off early in the morning, met the people, made the contract, returned to town, had my breakfast and stepped out on the porch, leaving my pistol in my room, when up rode Jolly to the edge of the sidewalk saying, "My name is Mance Jolly, the man you are looking for, now take me if you can." Then striking the spurs into his horse he galloped away.

That afternoon I visited another plantation of colored people and there witnessed one of the most revolting effects of the accursed institution of slavery that I have ever witnessed. The master called his slaves, about three hundred in number, up in line before the plantation house. When I asked him if his people were all present he replied, there is one more in the house, I'll get her out. Stepping inside the door he returned dragging by the hand a lovely, delicate girl about 19 years old, as white as any woman I ever saw. He roughly ordered her to take her place in line and as she passed by where I was standing said, "Father, I never knew that I was a nigger before." I said to this wretch that we call man, "Is that your child?" His reply was, "She is one of the house niggers."

I finished my duties on that plantation with all possible haste, leaving this human monster and his wretched people with feelings of indescribable disgust and utter loathing for a man who had become so degraded as to be guilty of such inhuman conduct, and longing for my term of service to end in this horrible place.

Next morning just as the guard had been mounted for the day, and the men whose duty it was to remain at the guard house had stacked arms, Jolly rode up alone to the guard saying, "Tell your colonel that unless he delivers my horse that his men stole from me at the meeting house on Sunday, I will kill him and every man in his regiment before they get out of this country." He wheeled his horse and rode away. The Sergeant of the guard commanded his men to take their guns and fire. Jolly laid over on the neck of his horse, which was running at full speed, the men after him, keeping up the fusillade until he was out of town. The horse was wounded and soon died, but the rider escaped.

That day's mail brought an order from Headquarters for me to turn over the command of the district to an Officer of the First Maine Infantry and proceed to Charleston and prepare to muster out my regiment whose term of service would soon expire. It required a few days to fetch in the outlying companies, which had been stationed throughout remote portions of the district and collect the numbers of cars necessary to transport the regiment and all their baggage. It was indeed a great relief to feel that I should soon be on my way homeward.

By Sept. 5th all was in readiness and we were busy all day loading the train and cooking rations or at least what we could obtain for our journey out of this wretched, unhappy, rebellious country. It was late in the afternoon when the train was ready to pull out. I was just stepping aboard ready to give the signal to the conductor to start when I saw a company of colored people coming from the town bearing what I thought was a stretcher containing a sick person. I waited for them, and when they reached the platform I found they were tenderly bearing a white Union Soldier of the 4th Ohio Cavalry.

He said, "They shot me (meaning the rebel soldiers) out of my saddle last April when we were scouting the country for Jeff Davis, took my horse and all I had, then left me alone to die. These kind colored people have nursed me and cared for me ever since. I had heard that you were leaving this country for the North and I begged them to fetch me to the train and I now ask you to take me with you. I have a wife and little ones living in Sandusky, Ohio. I want, if I can, to see them again before I die." I found that he had been shot through the neck, the ball injuring the spinal column so that his entire body below the shoulders was completely paralyzed and utterly helpless. I had him carried on to the train and laid him as carefully as we could in the aisle of the car.

Just as the men were doing this Mr. James L. Orr, with whom I had dined a few weeks before, came to the train and handed me the following letter commending my conduct while in command of the district, but the letter, which follows, speaks for itself.

> Anderson
> Sep 5th 1865
>
> Sir,
> Your command having been relieved from duty in the district it is due to you that I should express to you not only my own, but the sentiment of approval of the people of the Dept. at the manner in which you have discharged your duties as Commandant. The general sentiment of the public is that you have faithfully endeavored to do justice to all classes and conditions of society and in administering military law you have sought to extend impartial justice to all. You carry with you from here the personal wishes of the community for your personal and official success in life. I desire also to bear willing testimony to the kindness, courtesy and official integrity of Captain Sampson, Provost Marshal and Lieutenant White, Adjutant, who have so ably seconded you in your administration of the department.
>
> I am sir
> Very respectfully yours
> James L. Orr

Mr. Orr told me in a whisper that since writing that letter he had been put in possession of information that led him to believe that my entire regiment would be annihilated before we could get out of the country. He could not upon his life give the plot away as it would cost him his life if it should be known that he had ever mentioned it to me. But said he, "In token of my friendship for you I will give you this pistol that I have carried for many years to defend yourself with," handing me a fine ivory handled pistol that had been in his possession during his sojourn in Washington when he was Speaker of the House of Representatives before the war; and likewise Colonel of the 7th S.C. Infantry in the Confederate Army as well as his companion in the Confederate Senate. He said whether you live to get to Charleston or not, all the plans we have agreed upon for the future shall be faithfully carried out on my part. Bidding me good night he hurried away.

I well knew that his warning to me meant danger ahead; so made my plans to meet whatever might turn up. I had a little black Sergeant whose name was Fred Brown of Co. D, a man of splendid nerve and every inch a soldier. I handed him the pistol and told him to take four men of his company with him on the engine and if he saw anything that looked suspicious on the part of the man who was holding the throttle to blow his head off. I then gave the signal for the train to pull out, not knowing of course what danger we might meet at any moment.

Night had covered the earth with darkness which much increased the intensity of the situation. We had not made over two miles of our journey when we had to cross a trestle bridge about 115 ft high over a running stream of water. When we had reached the middle of the bridge some one pulled the coupling pin and the engine ran away leaving the entire train at a standstill. Then a sharp volley of musketry was opened on the cars from both banks of the ravine. Our men were prevented from returning the fire, or in any way defending themselves as the men could not leave the cars as there was no room beside the train to stand on, and darkness so completely shut us in that we were entirely at the mercy of our foes. I remember having said to myself if Sergeant Brown is yet alive he will come to our relief.

We had not long to wait before we heard, above the rattle of musketry, the welcome sound of the engine backing down, and the coupling pin was dropped in and we were pulled out of the fight. When the engine struck the train, Brown's pistol was at the ear of the engineer who had been in the plot for our destruction but had been discovered by the little black sergeant, the hero who had the true instinct of a soldier to act with that kind of intelligent bravery at the proper time to save the lives of the entire regiment which would have been wholly annihilated; as the plot was as I afterwards learned, to set fire to the bridge and destroy the train and everyone on board.

During the remainder of our journey to Newberry, the end of the railroad line, that Johnny Reb Engineer received his orders from Sergeant Brown. I have often thought that when the impartial historian shall sit down to write the story of the neglected heroes of the great war for freedom, that he will devote at least one page to this noble black soldier whose conduct on this occasion should give him an honored place among the world's gallant men. Then perhaps the millions of American people who read his story will hang their heads in shame when they recall the fact that this hero and his comrades who remained in the South were disfranchised and debarred from the right of American citizenship by the same class of people who were the prime movers in this dastardly attempt at the wholesale murder of my regiment months after Lee had surrendered the last of the rebel Army and the perpetrators of this crime are enjoying the privileges of full citizenship.

When we were safely out of our affair on the bridge I went to look after the poor wounded white soldier and found him quite cheerful. He said this is the first fight I have been in for four years that I could not take a hand in. When we arrived at Newberry we were obliged to leave the poor fellow with the colored people that had been his benefactors since the day he was wounded as we had no ambulance in which to transport one so severely wounded from Newberry to Columbia. The railroad between these points not having been repaired since Sherman destroyed it on his march to Raleigh in the February before. I never heard of him after we parted at Newberry.

Upon our arrival at Columbia we had hoped to receive fresh supplies of rations, enough to carry us to the end of our journey, but we found that at the earnest request of the Andrew Johnson government or misgovernment at Washington, the General commanding the department had released the military control of the only R.R. reaching that city and turned it over to the former owners. As they had no love for Yankee soldiers and found it quite to their advantage to decline to transport army rations while there were so many things needed for the rebuilding of the wilderness that Sherman had left after his march through the Carolinas.

I found the 25th Ohio Infantry were stationed at the post and when I made requisition for rations to feed my men there was but 3/4 lbs of salt pork per man including the Ohio troops. The Colonel commanding refused to let me have a single ration. I at once told him that my men were on the verge of starvation and I would have my portion or I would take it by force. This brought him to terms and just three quarters of a pound of salt pork per man was secured for the regiment. On this I commenced my march to Orangeburg, thirty-two miles away. I compelled the men to eat the pork without cooking it as I knew if it was cooked it would not satisfy their hunger. We started on our march; the weather was awfully hot and nothing in sight to eat short of the 32 mile march. But this was my only hope for relief and off we started on a race for life.

After making about ten miles we reached a plantation house. I halted the men in a piece of woods for a rest and to wait till the cool of the afternoon. The owner of the place came to me and said that he had but two hogs left on his plantation and implored me to see that they were not killed. He invited me to dine with him, which I gladly did.

While at the dinner table a colored servant came and said to mine host that the soldiers wanted to borrow the big iron kettle that he had for boiling sugar cane in as they wanted to make coffee in it. The planter looked at me and I at him, but of course I said not a word. The boys got the loan of the kettle; I got a cornbread dinner and left the house with as little ceremony as possible. I rejoined the regiment where the coffee was being made, but upon close inspection I found that fresh pork instead of coffee was boiling at a furious rate. I asked no questions but gave the men the time to finish their cooking, return the kettle with thanks and off we started for another long hard hungry march.

By dark I found we had made about fifteen miles or covered half the distance from Columbia to the point where we could get rations. I found the men were weary and exhausted so I halted for the night at a farm house, the planter agreeing to furnish the Officers only with supper at a dollar each, permitting them to lie on the floor in his house provided I would detail a strong guard to protect his sweet potato field so that his potatoes should not be disturbed. I ordered Co. K to be properly posted around the field with orders to shoot anybody that might molest the growing crop.

I then turned in for a sleep and almost every half hour during the early part of the night a shot was fired and the old planter would awaken me to say, "Them was mighty good guards as they were shooting someone all the time." I thought, you don't know Co. K as well as I do. I think there were about thirty officers that ate supper and paid their dollar for his cornbread and sorghum and for the privilege of sleeping on the hard floor for a part of the night. We paid him more good money than he had probably seen since Sumter was fired upon in April of '61; and with it he could purchase more real comforts than he had since the war began. I did not take the time to look over the potato patch nor did I care to even if there had been daylight to do so, but I'll venture to say there was not a single potato left in his field notwithstanding the vigilance of Co. K.

A little while after midnight we sounded the reveille, the regiment fell into line and we began our march through a sandy, barren pine country with a very small supply of water. By ten o'clock that morning the men began to fall out exhausted and laid down by the roadside. We had eleven miles yet to go before food could be had. I became quite alarmed lest many of them should perish from starvation. I was just to my wits end to arouse them sufficiently without resorting to cruelty to finish the march to where supplies could be secured.

'Tis said that "Music hath charms" and knowing that we had a company cook by the name of Jim Lercy, a fat jolly fellow belonging to Co. C who could play the fiddle, I thought I would try the power of music with these weary tired men whose love for music was almost a ruling passion. I ordered Jim to mount my horse, so with camp cooking utensils, saucepans, coffee pots all strapped to his back with the fiddle on top of all, he mounted; took the fiddle and soon the notes of the instrument was wafted on the wings of the gentle breeze back to the men lying prostrate by the roadside.

As they heard the old tunes which Jim had played around the campfires in the happier days of our regimental life, they began to forget their fatigue and in a very short time everyone was on his feet and marching with a new impulse and energy that was marvelous to behold. Surely the wonderful power of music to transform a regiment of tired, weary, exhausted, and hungry men into hilarious joyous soldiers who completed those last eleven miles of their march with mirth and joyousness was demonstrated as never before. I shall always believe that Jim Lercy's fiddle and my horse saved many a life that day. The men used to say, "Only for de fiddle and de horse we would all hab died in de wilderness." We finished our wearisome march before nightfall; a good supper was cooked and eaten; and all the men were safely encamped and enjoyed the much needed sleep and rest.

From Orangeburg we took the cars for Charleston where we were ordered to take command of the forts in Charleston Harbor, with headquarters at Battery Wagner on Morris Island, in front of whose frowning ramparts we had spent so many weary months the year before while they were still in the hands of the Confederacy. Here by a single fate of war it was our fortune to end our Army life as a regiment in the month of February following.

When the different companies of the regiment had been assigned to the several stations on the Islands and in the forts in the harbor including Moultrie, Sumter and Castle Pinckney, I was allowed twenty days leave of absence and went North to meet the dear ones from whom I had been separated so long. I left full instructions in a quiet way to give as many of the men as could be spared from duty a short leave of absence to look after the interests of Mr. Orr, whom we had set our hearts upon making Governor at the coming fall election.

Here I want to record the fact that I followed General Daniel E. Sickles in command, who, upon our report of the conduct of the railroad officials in refusing or neglecting to transport government rations, seized all the railroads of the state and compelled all other kinds of freight to be withheld until the army in his department had been fully supplied. I always admired this grand old comrade for this action and whenever we meet at national G.A.R. encampments we always speak of the days when we served together in the Carolinas.

One company of the regiment was stationed at the jail in the city of Charleston and on my return from my leave of absence; I found that we had three white men as prisoners for the murder of six members of the 1st Maine Regt. that had relieved me at Anderson only the month before.

One of them was Crawford Keyes, the man between whom he and his former slaves I had made the contract at the time I took the old Sheriff with me. He was charged, in connection with his son and another man, with having killed the detachment of Soldiers, who were guarding a flat boat loaded with cotton at the headwaters of the Savannah River and attempting to run it down the river to Augusta for the purpose of selling it. The murder was discovered and the men were caught with the boat and cargo in their possession.

The proof of their guilt was thoroughly established at the trial held in Charleston. They were convicted on Thursday; on Friday General Sickles approved the finding of the Court and ordered their execution on Saturday. But all South Carolina had the ear of Andrew Johnson and he telegraphed a respite and ordered them sent to Darlington to be tried by a jury of their peers. Of course they were acquitted and soon returned to their homes in Anderson Co. I heard years afterward that the two younger men had died and that the old slave master, the leader in this foul murder was still living but stone blind and leading a life of wretched poverty and disgrace.

Nearly all of the few months that remained of my Army life was spent promoting the election of Mr. James Orr to the governorship of what we hoped would prove reconstructed South Carolina. In the month of

November the state election was held under the Reconstruction Act and to our great joy my esteemed friend was elected governor of South Carolina.

He came to Charleston on his way to Columbia to be inaugurated. I together with Sergeant Brown called on him at the Mills House. After a most cordial greeting Sergeant Brown returned to the new Governor of South Carolina the pistol which he had given me at the depot at Anderson Courthouse the night we left that town and which was used with such good effect in the fight on the trestle bridge.

While we were making out our final muster out rolls we received word that General Grant was coming to visit Charleston and the forts in the harbor so we spent some time in cleaning up the companies and preparing the garrison to receive the general. He arrived accompanied by Gen. Sickles and staff who dressed in full uniform with all the splendor of gold lace & shining accoutrements, while the General of all the Armies of the Union was in plain citizen's dress. Here at Fort Sumter I had the distinguished honor of meeting the man who led our Armies to victory for the first time in my life.

I had a man in Co. I by the name of Rochenbaugh, the most un-soldierly looking man in the regiment, but an excellent company cook. I was so anxious that he be kept out of sight that I ordered him kept in the cook house in the bomb proof where General Grant would not see him.

To my chagrin and utter dismay as soon as the General came on shore, and had acknowledged the salute of the companies that had been drawn up to receive him, as I took his arm to escort him over the Fort, he insisted upon seeing where the food was cooked. In spite of my efforts to steer him away from the cook house, he made straight for it. The first thing his eyes met was this ungainly soldier that I had tried to keep hidden from him. With a most awkward attempt at a military salute he received the commander in chief of all the Armies of the Union, who after complimenting him upon the cleanliness of his cook house and cooking utensils bade him good day, and said to me, Colonel, we will now see the fort.

After a leisurely walk over the battered and battle torn ramparts of that historic fortification where the first shot was fired and the war began, he said his time was up and he would bid me good day. My officers asked me to request him to leave his autograph for them. He cheerfully complied, and seating himself at a table he wrote his name six times, one for each officer present. As soon as he had left a contention arose as to who should keep the pen he had used. I settled the matter by keeping it myself as a souvenir of our first meeting with General Grant.

From this time on our attention was fully occupied with preparing the muster out rolls of the regiment until Feb 9th 1866 on which date, standing as nearly as we could ascertain on the grave of that gallant young hero, Col. Robt. G. Shaw of the 54th Mass. Colored Regiment, who fell at the head of his regiment on the night of July 18 1863 and who was buried in the same graves with his niggers; as was stated in the Charleston papers of the next day, I issued the following farewell order to my regiment.

Headquarters 33rd USCT
Late 1st So Car. Volunteers
Morris Island S.C.
Feb 9th 1866

Comrades;
The hour is at hand when we must separate forever, and nothing can ever take from us the pride we feel when we look back upon the history of the 1st South Carolina Volunteers—the first black regiment that ever bore arms in defense of freedom on the Continent of America.

On the 9th day of May 1862 at which time there were nearly four millions of your race in a bondage sanctioned by the laws of the land and protected by our flag; on that day in the face of floods of prejudice that well nigh deluged every avenue to manhood and true liberty, you came forth to do battle for your country and your kindred.

For long and weary months without pay or even the privilege of being recognized as soldiers, you labored on, only to be disbanded and sent to your homes, without even a hope of reward. And when our country, necessitated by the deadly struggle with armed traitors, finally granted you the opportunity again to come forth in defense of the nation's life, the alacrity with which you responded to the call gave abundant evidence of your readiness to strike a manly blow for the liberty of your race. And from that little band of hopeful trusting and brave men, who gathered at Camp Saxton on Port Royal Island in the fall of 1862 amongst the terrible prejudices surrounding us has grown an army of a Hundred and Eighty Six Thousand black soldiers, whose valor and heroism has won for your race a name which will live as long as the undying pages of history shall endure; and by whose efforts united with those of the white man, armed rebellion has been conquered, the millions of bondsmen have been emancipated, and the fundamental law of the land has been so altered as to remove forever the possibility of human slavery being re-established within the borders of redeemed America.

The flag of our land restored to its rightful significance now floats over every foot of our territory from Maine to California and beholds only Freemen. The prejudices, which formerly existed against you, are all well nigh rooted out. Soldiers you have done your duty and acquitted yourselves like men, who, activated by such ennobling motives could not fail; and as the results of your fidelity and obedience you have won your freedom. And oh how great the reward!

It seems fitting to me that the last hours of our existence should be passed amidst the unmarked graves of your comrades at Fort Wagner. Near you rest the bones of Colonel Shaw buried by an enemy's hand in the grave with his black soldiers who fell by his side, where in the future your children's children will come on pilgrimages to do homage to the ashes of those that fell in this glorious struggle.

The flag which was presented to us by the Rev. George B. Cheever and his congregation of New York City on the 1st of January 1863—The day when Lincoln's immortal proclamation of freedom was given to the world—and which you have borne so nobly through the war, is now to be rolled up forever and deposited in our Nations Capital. And while there it shall rest with the battles in which you have participated inscribed upon its folds, it will be a source of pride to us all to remember that it has never been disgraced by a cowardly faltering in the hour of danger or polluted by a traitor's touch.

Now that you are to lay aside your arms and return to the peaceful avocations of life, I adjure you, by the association and history of the past, and the love you bear for your liberties, to harbor no feelings of hatred toward your former masters, but to seek in the paths of honesty, virtue, sobriety and industry, and by a willing obedience to the laws of the land, to grow up to the full stature of American citizens.

The church, the schoolhouse, and the right to be forever free are now secured to you and every prospect before you is full of hope and encouragement. The nation guarantees to you full protection and justice, and will require from you in return, that respect for the laws and orderly deportment which will prove to everyone your right to all the privileges of freemen.

To the officers of the regiment I would say; your toils are ended, your mission is fulfilled, and we separate forever. The fidelity, patience and patriotism with which you have discharged your duties to your men and to your country entitle you to a far higher tribute than any words of thankfulness which I can give you from the bottom of my heart. You will find your reward in the proud conviction that the cause for which you have battled so nobly has been crowned with abundant success.

Officers and Soldiers of the 33 U.S. Colored Troops once the First South Carolina Volunteers, I bid you farewell.

By order of
Lt. Col. C.T. Trowbridge
Commanding Regiment

E.W. Hyde
1st Lieut. 33rd U.S.C.T. and acting Adjutant

After the regiment was discharged, I remained in service until March 15th 1866, settling my accounts and on that date I received my honorable discharge, which was signed by General Charles Devens, one of Massachusetts's most distinguished soldiers. I took off the Union blue and hurried to my Northern home, after more than four years of service in the war.

I took my place once more in the ranks of private citizenship and endeavored to make my way in the business world with thousands of others, who, like myself had abandoned our all at home to enter the army when the country called us to the field of war. During the maudlin, vacillating my-policy administration of Andrew Johnson the struggle for a foothold in the race of life for the returned Union soldiers was not altogether one of pleasure or profit, but this unfortunate and miserable administration drew to an end. And the American people once more called the hero that had led us to victory in war. Called him to the chair of the chief executive head of our nation. Our hopes revived and things went more smoothly with the soldier citizen.

With the end of the Johnson regime, came also the end of the term of office of Gov. Orr of South Carolina, who had honestly and faithfully tried to administer the affairs of his office, so that justice might be done to all classes. He received little or no encouragement from the old slave master inhabitants of the state, who, in place of coming to his aid, taking a leading part in the politics of the state, and helping to so shape the affairs that reconstruction would be all its citizens had hoped for, sulked in their tents and did all that lay in their power to hinder and discourage the Governor to the end of his term at which time he came out of office completely ostracized socially and politically, and much depressed and discouraged.

When this condition was made known to Gen. Grant he appointed him Minister to St. Petersburg, Russia where he died. His body was sent home for burial, it was laid in state in the rotunda of the City Hall in New York. I was permitted to see the encoffined form of my old friend who had befriended me in the Confederate senate, who had lent me his pistol to defend my life with when a soldier in the far off mountains of South Carolina. I doubt of any one of the vast throng who viewed the lifeless remains of that grand old southern gentleman on that occasion knew how James L. Orr came to receive his appointment as minister to St. Petersburg as well as I did.

The story of my experiences with a Negro regiment in the Freedman's Bureau would not be complete if I neglected to say that I have twice met and had a reunion with Sergeant Brown since the close of the war. The first time was in 1884 when on a steamer returning from a trip to the sunny land of Florida by way of Port Royal.

From the deck, I saw among a large gang of colored men who were loading cotton, my little black hero. I hastened on shore, we recognized each other and in a moment he threw his arms around me, and the reunion was such as only old comrades can understand who have braved danger together in days long gone by. But this meeting soon ended as it required but a few moments for the freight to be put on board. The steamer put out to sea and I, from the upper deck waved a good bye to one of the most heroic soldiers that I had under my command.

The passengers had noticed me and the meeting on the wharf. Two young ladies, who seemed inclined to attract attention, took occasion as they strolled past where I stood, to say, so that the bystanders could hear them; Did you see that old white man kiss that nigger? I turned upon them and said with all the scorn I could inject into my looks and action, young ladies, if you had had the experience that I had once with that black man you would know a good thing when you meet and kiss it too. I told the passengers the story of the night on the trestle bridge with the negro I had just left on the wharf. I was from that time until we reached New York a kind of lion on deck while the simple young women sought the seclusion of their state room and we saw no more of them.

Six years later I happened to be in Beaufort, S.C. and made diligent inquiry for Sergeant Brown. I learned he was very sick at his house a few miles out of town; taking a carriage, I soon arrived at his home and found him sitting near the ashes of his smoldering fire, suffering from a severe attack of dropsy with feet dreadfully swollen and quite feeble nearing the end of life's journey, but glad indeed to meet me once again. After leaving some means with which to add to his comfort, I bade him a soldier's farewell.

Returning to Beaufort where as many of the old members of the regiment as could be found were holding a Campfire, I made arrangements with them to care tenderly for our Comrade Brown until his march of life should be ended and then to see that his remains were borne with military honors to the National Cemetery close by the town of Beaufort; requesting them to send the bill to me for settlement. One more will thus be added to the 9,241 dead heroes that sleep under the pine and cypress in the southland until the final reveille is sounded and the march of Eternity is begun.

In closing the story of my soldier life in the Freedman's Bureau I will detain my readers just long enough to say: when the national Republican convention met in Minneapolis that nominated Benjamin Harrison for the second time for President I had the pleasure of meeting the delegates from Anderson County, S.C., some of whom admitted that they participated in the attack on my regiment at the trestle bridge and that Mance Jolly who planned the attack was compelled, because of his lawlessness in S.C. after the army had been withdrawn, to leave the state. He went to Texas and there after being detected in some crime for which the Officers of the law were pursuing him, hoping to escape capture by jumping into a stream and swimming to the opposite shore, was drowned. His body was never recovered, but no doubt—furnished food for the fish of the sea.

After the war, Trowbridge returned to New York and was a four-term alderman from the 10th Ward of Brooklyn. In April 1882, he moved to Minneapolis, Minnesota, where he became the custodian of the old Minnesota capitol building until his death on Christmas Eve, 1907. The governor of Minnesota ordered the flag flown at half-staff and the capitol building closed on the day of his funeral.

For years after the war, Colonel Trowbridge sought to locate the 33rd's regimental flag. He found that it had been shipped to Washington and was stored there with all the rest of the battle flags of the U.S. Colored Troops that fought in the Civil War.

Through the "kindness of an officer of the War Department," Trowbridge wrote, he was able to secure a star from the flag. "The dear old flag!" he wrote. "There let it rest in peaceful serenity as long as my country shall endure. My comrades, who fought under it, where are they? With most of them, 'It is all quiet along the Potomac tonight, no sound save the rush of the river. Soft falls the dew on the face of the dead. My comrades are off duty forever.' "

Bibliography

Dyer, Frederick H. *A Compendium of the War of the Rebellion, Vol. II.* Des Moines: Dyer Publishing Company. Dayton, OH: Morningside Press, 1908.

Glatthaar, Joseph T. *The Civil War Alliance of Black Soldiers and White Officers.* New York: The Free Press, 1990.

Higginson, Col. Thomas Wentworth. *Trowbridge obituary.* Boston: *Boston Transcript,* 1907.

Higginson, Col. Thomas Wentworth. *Army Life in a Black Regiment.* Boston: Osgood and Company, 1870.

Payne, Daniel Alexander. *Recollections of Seventy Years.* Nashville: Publication House of the A.M.E. Sunday School Union, 1888.

Romero, Patricia W. *Susie King Taylor, A Black Woman's Civil War Memoirs.* Princeton, NJ: Markus Wiener Publishers, Inc., 1988.

Taylor, Susie King. *Reminiscences of my life in camp with the 33rd U.S. Colored Troops, late 1st South Carolina Volunteers.* Boston, 1902.

The War of the Rebellion: A Compilation of the Official Records of the Union and Confederate Armies. Washington: Government Printing Office, 1880–1901.

Trowbridge, Charles T. *Experiences in the Freedmen's Bureau.* Trowbridge Papers, Minnesota Historical Society.

Trowbridge, Charles T. *A Star from my Regimental Flag.*

Trowbridge, Francis B. *Trowbridge's in America.* New Haven, CT: Higginson Publishing Company, 1908.